THE SECOND

FACE

By

Missionary Susie D. Liddell

Copyright © 2026, Missionary Susie D. Liddell

All Rights Reserved

Any unauthorized reproduction or use of this material is strictly forbidden. No part of this book may be reproduced or transmitted in any form or by any means, whether electronic or mechanical, such as photocopying, recording, or through any information storage and retrieval system, without explicit written consent from the author.

We have made every reasonable effort to ensure the accuracy of the information presented in this publication. However, the author accepts no responsibility for any errors or omissions that may occur.

ISBN:

Paperback: 978-1-971141-23-7

Hardcover: 978-1-971141-24-4

DEDICATION

To my Lord and Savior, Jesus Christ, the One who turned my pain into purpose and my tears into testimony. To every reader whose heart beats between these pages, may you find healing, forgiveness, and a reason to smile again. And may you wear the face that your heart is feeling, for God sees the heart behind every expression.

May your face always reflect the love of God, your heart stay open to His mercy, and your life be a living example of His grace.

To every mother or father who has lost a child, always take your pain to the presence of God. Find someone you can talk to, a good therapist, but never forget about God. There you will find comfort, peace, and strength to endure.

To my beloved husband, Smith Liddell Jr, my sons Smith Liddell III and Justin L. Wright, who is with Jesus, and my daughter Brittney Wright, thank you for your love, your prayers, and your strength. You are a part of this story and of every face that shines through it—here on earth and in heaven.

To my Faith Temple Complex Church of God in Christ family, thank you for your prayers, encouragement, and unwavering love. You have stood by me through the journey, and I thank God for every one of you.

ACKNOWLEDGMENTS

I want to thank GOD, who gave me the knowledge, wisdom, and understanding to write this book. Every word, every chapter, and every revelation came through divine guidance, and I give God all the glory for it.

To every reader who has taken the time to read The Second Face, I thank you from the depths of my heart. May this book touch your spirit, lift your soul, and remind you that God can turn any pain into purpose.

Let God heal you wherever you hurt.

May the lessons shared within these pages help you uncover truth, walk in mercy, and live with hope.

With love and gratitude, Missionary Susie D. Liddell

I also thank my mother, Alice West, who prayed for me through every trial and never stopped believing in me.

TABLE OF CONTENTS

DEDICATION .... *i*

ACKNOWLEDGMENTS .... *ii*

Chapter 1 The Face of Goodness *1*

Chapter 2 The Man behind the Mask *8*

Chapter 3 The Woman behind the Mask *15*

Chapter 4 Tiara's Awakening *21*

Chapter 5 The New Me *26*

Chapter 6 The Face Is Exposed *29*

Chapter 7 A Face of Hope *36*

Chapter 8 The Face of Truth *44*

Chapter 9 The Face of Mercy *54*

Chapter 10 The Face of Blessing *62*

Chapter 11 The Reunion of Grace *73*

Closing Prayer By Missionary Susie D. Liddell *80*

Final Reflection *82*

Page Left Blank Intentionally

Chapter 1

The Face of Goodness

Listening to raindrops echoing off shutters on a chilly November morning, a day that seemed normal at first, turned into the worst nightmare of a person's life, a day they could never have imagined. Francine woke early, starting her day with prayer and preparing for work, wanting to look her best.

Suddenly, she received a call that her son had been killed. Her heart sank, and she felt her identity shattered. She continued to go to work each day as she had before. At the office, she masked her pain with a smile, performed her duties, and tried to reflect God's love and Jesus's presence. Yet beneath the surface, every breath felt heavier.

Each routine moment, pouring coffee, greeting coworkers, became a quiet test of endurance. No one around her could see that her heart was silently screaming for the comfort only God could give. But on the inside, she was broke. She came home, followed her daily routine, which included cooking, cleaning, and taking care of her family. But on the inside, she was shattered. This happened day after day, night after night. She cried so hard that eventually her tears dried up. Her family didn't understand, didn't know, because she had a smile on her face. Deep down, she was broke.

This was the first time she thought, I can just die. She felt, What is the point in going on? she asked in her mind. Why am I still here? She pondered those things in her heart. Later, the Lord responded: "You have a job to do. You have souls to win. Remember, your family needs you." Tears streamed down Francine's thin face. It was hard for her to enjoy a meal, knowing what had happened to her dear son.

The Word of the Lord came to Francine one morning in prayer, saying, in a still, comforting voice, *Lo, I am with you always, even to the end of the world. You will see your son again. Get up. Straighten your face. Put on the whole armor of God. Walk worthy of your calling. Replace the pain with goodness. Do good. Love. Live this life that you're required to do. You can be sad, but know that I am with you.* Those divine words settled deep in her spirit, filling her broken heart with a quiet strength she had not felt in a long time. From that day to the next day, Francine began to trust God with all her heart. She began to open her heart wider and pour out the love of God that was on the inside. She replaced that pain that was in her, never forgetting her beloved son, but turning that memory into a sacred space, a place of worship and reflection where she could continually feel God's presence. And from that day to the next day, Francine began to understand the whole purpose for which she had to suffer. Anytime she had heard that a mother had lost her child or was suffering in that same capacity, she poured into them with compassion, making gentle phone calls, visiting their homes, and offering every word of comfort her soul could give, or whatever she could put her hands to do, mainly talking to them and praying and encouraging them to know that God is not forgotten.

So she used that love and service as a weapon to defeat her pain. Francine's journey to transparency came from forgiveness, a forgiveness that did not come easily, but one that bloomed through prayer and surrender to God's will.

The person who took her son's life, she realized that true forgiveness comes from the heart. She began to pray for the very person who caused her the heartbreak of her life. She felt as if her heart was broken into a million pieces. But she had enough love on the inside to see the soul of the person who did this unforgivable act. But she knew she had to do this. Because of this, this is how we reach Chapter 1, the face of goodness. Forgiveness is the reason that she could have this face of goodness.

Because she knows that God is good and everything He does is wonderful, she finds comfort in Jesus, our perfect example of goodness. Jesus shed His blood on the cross, demonstrating the incredible goodness of God. Francine had to deliver a victim impact statement, which touched the hearts of her family's advocate. She shared that she felt touched and blessed in her soul because of Francine's heartfelt testimony and her prayers for her son's killer. She saw forgiveness in a way she had never witnessed before. To this day, Francine and her advocates remain lifelong friends. This is a beautiful example of how God can show us His goodness.

After Francine spoke, the judge sentenced the murderer to 50 years in prison. Yet, I felt a deep sense of peace because I knew we had done our part by forgiving him. We prayed for his salvation and hoped he would find the Lord in his heart. That was our sincere prayer for him.

After the sentence was dropped, people were getting done, and the court was over, I ran into a police officer. He said, Ma'am, Ma'am, I have something to tell you. I stopped. I said, Yes, sir. He said, Ma'am, if you were there, you could have seen the peace that was on your son's face. I was there at the scene after your son was killed. And he had so much peace, I just could not believe it. So rest easy. The peace of God was all over his face. After court, and after everything was said and done, we had eaten our dinner, and the day was fully spent. Right before bed, I got on my knees and gave God the glory, telling Him, Thank you for peace that surpasses all understanding. Thank you for loving me enough that you gave me peace with this situation. My entire family, my husband, and my children were at peace, knowing that God is always in control. There's nothing hard for Him, nothing too big, nothing too wide. He's superior over all things. And we don't understand His ways, but one day, we will see Him and know all.

Many years have gone by since that terrible day. A day we will never forget. As I mentioned earlier, that day shattered my heart into a million pieces. Part of my heart was taken then, but we continue to live and trust that we will see him again. He is never forgotten. Every holiday, every birthday, we keep him in our thoughts. During vacations, we ask, What would Justin be doing right now? He would make this trip even more special because of the love we had for him. Francine could talk to her daughter about anything, and she shared how her heart just ached and hurt. She placed her hand on her chest, not fully understanding the grief process. All she knew was that she felt pain inside, and she was hollow. Part of her heart had been ripped out. Her daughter said, "It's okay, Mom. We are both hurting, but we will get through this together. The love we share will guide us through anything. And God's love for us is beyond measure, unmatched." She hugged her mother and kissed her on the cheek. She said, "Life will get better. Better days are coming. Believe that." Francine's husband entered the room and asked, "What are you girls talking about?"

He truly understood. He was just trying to lighten the mood. He was hurting too, but he didn't talk about his grief, not with me. He always tried to protect me and keep me from crying. While on the inside, he cried day and night. But we as a family prayed together, talked together, and stayed together. Francine's unbearable grief turned into months of healing through God's love. Francine's local church had named a Ministry J club. It stands for loving Jesus and remembering Justin, after her son, and each year, they are educating children, getting them ready for the next level of care. The Lord provided a way for Francine to always remember her son through love, through ministry, and through giving. Over time, Francine began to see how God used her pain to bless others. Every act of kindness she offered became a seed of healing in someone else's life and in her own. It was in giving that she truly found restoration.

Through her late pastor and her current pastor, they are a blessing. God began to speak. He said, Remember that message I gave you? Don't cease to praise me. There was a reason for that. I was making you stronger. Building up your faith. You said, You will bless the Lord at all times. And that my praises shall continually be in your mouth. This is the opportunity that you have to prove to me. Prove what you've been saying all this time. She carried her pain to God's presence. The face of goodness was displayed with a smile. At the end, it turned out to be the true face of goodness through the loving and sharing of Jesus Christ. The pain was displayed in Francine's mind and in her heart, which was on the inside. Now, the face of goodness is truly a face of goodness because it's the love of Jesus Christ. And in that love, Francine finally found her freedom, the peace that only comes from knowing Jesus is still good, even in the hardest seasons.

Francine became a missionary in the Grand OLE Church of God in Christ. She thanked God on that day as she gazed into the crowd to see her son and her daughter cheering her on. Francine realized she did have a purpose. She had children who loved her, along with a husband right by her side.

Chapter 2

The Man behind the Mask

Jonathan was born in a time of deep sorrow and uncertainty. He had witnessed several tragic drug deals that went bad, and the tension of police brutality was rising across the nation.

For lack of a better word, he was emotionally and mentally broken. Jonathan was raised by his father, who tried to provide the best he knew how for his four sons. He worked a nine-to-five job and sometimes worked nights to care for them. Jonathan's mother had died when he was young, and his father would pray many nights with weary eyes, asking that the Lord would send him strength and help. One night, the Lord spoke to Jonathan's father's heart and told him not to go to work that Sunday. Obediently, the father called his job and told them he would not be there.

Early the next morning, he rose and called out, "Children! Jonathan, where are you?" Everyone came out except Jonathan. His father went to Jonathan's room, but he wasn't there. An hour passed, and the father began to get dressed for church.

When Jonathan finally came in, his father asked, "Where were you?" Jonathan said, "Why are you here? I thought you'd be at work." His father asked again, and Jonathan reached into his pocket, pulling out a bundle of money. "Dad," he said, "I've been working some nights because I want to help you." His father was overcome with emotion and embraced him with tears streaming down his face. The other children were moved to tears when they saw the love between them. Jonathan was a good brother and a good son. In that simple moment, the father saw God's answer to his prayers a glimpse of hope through his son's heart. After breakfast, the family got ready for church. They walked across the field to a small church that had been there for generations, its white paint slightly faded by time but rich with history and love. The place was filled with memories, songs echoing through the wooden beams, laughter that once filled the pews, and moments of heartbreak that still lingered in the walls. When they entered, their hearts were filled with emotions. They remembered their mother singing in the choir, her voice rising with joy as she danced across the wooden floor, testifying about the goodness and mercy of God.

It was also the last place they had seen her, their wife and mother, laid to rest beneath the same roof where she had once praised the Lord. The father realized then why he had avoided church for so long. He couldn't face the pain of losing her. But that day, the call of God was stronger than his fear. Suddenly, the preacher's voice broke through his thoughts: "God sees you! He loves you so much!" The father looked up with tears in his eyes. He stood and cried, "I surrender. I surrender. I hear You, Lord. I know you love me. I know you didn't forget about me. Help us." In that sacred moment, his voice broke through years of silence and pain, echoing like a cry from a wounded heart finally finding peace. The congregation broke into praise, and the atmosphere shifted. Hands lifted, tears flowed, and faith filled the room. The sanctuary erupted with worship, as if heaven itself had bent low to rejoice with them..

After the service, the pastor greeted the congregation, hugging the father and his children. "I never gave up on you all," he said warmly. "I've been praying this whole time. See you next Sunday." That afternoon, the family gathered around the dinner table. The familiar smell of home-cooked food could not hide the emptiness left behind. They talked about how much they missed their mother and how hard it was to face her loss. Each word was heavy, but every tear that fell drew them a little closer together. None of them wanted to admit how deep the pain ran. Jonathan tried to talk about it, but couldn't. It had been two years since her death, but it still felt like yesterday.

Jonathan, the oldest, quietly made a promise to himself that day to protect his family, to honor his mother's memory, and to never let grief destroy what remained. He studied hard, made straight A's, and became valedictorian of his class. His dedication was not driven solely by ambition but by love and a sense of responsibility. He went to an Ivy League college and earned a bachelor's degree in the arts. Over time, he became a world-class actor recognized on screens across the globe, admired for his grace and humility as much as for his talent. He was handsome, well-spoken, and charming. People admired him.

His father was proud, often showing others his son's movies and interviews. "That's my boy," he'd say with pride, his eyes glistening with joy. Jonathan kept his promise; he retired his father, bought him a new house, and ensured his brothers received a good education. He had fulfilled his mother's dream for them, a family restored, standing strong in faith and success.

A few years later, Jonathan married a beautiful woman, one of his co-workers. For a time, life was radiant; love and laughter filled their home, and they dreamed of a future that felt unshakable. They had a wonderful life until life's storms arrived quietly, eroding what they had built together. Their marriage ended in divorce, but they had a son, Jonathan Jr. Like his father, he was tall, handsome, and intelligent. The bond between them was strongly rooted in admiration, love, and the shared weight of expectation.

He became a popular YouTube influencer known as "Black Trump," and his audience adored him, helping his followers grow into the millions. However, Jonathan Sr. didn't feel comfortable with the content his son was creating. He gently advised, "Son, you need to do better. It's disrespectful." Jonathan Jr. brushed it off with a casual shrug, saying, "It's just entertainment, Dad." As his fame increased, so did the risks involved.

After mocking the President on his channel one night, Jonathan Jr. began receiving threats. His father called him again, saying, "Son, tone it down. It's too much." Jonathan Jr. said, "It's okay, Dad. I got this." One night, after filming a video, Jonathan Jr. was attacked in his car and lost his life. When his father found out, his world shattered. He rushed to his son's workplace, saw his car, and found his lifeless body inside. The scream that came from him could only be understood by a parent who has lost a child. It was the beginning of Jonathan's dark descent. Jonathan tried to cope, but he drowned in grief. He tried therapy, prayer, and work, but nothing helped. He started drinking heavily and taking antidepressants. He tried to numb the pain.

Even though he attended church and smiled for the cameras, inside, he was falling apart. The world saw a man who had everything, but at home, he was a man lost behind a mask. The man behind the mask was drowning. His success couldn't fill the emptiness. He talked to God while drinking, tears streaming down his face. "Why, Lord? Why my son? I've done everything right!" But God did hear him. Jonathan died, but he saw the face of God and walked into a new light. He was restored. What the enemy meant for evil, God turned into good. The entertainment world was devastated. They held a memorial service in his honor. His younger brother delivered the eulogy, speaking of Jonathan's kindness and love. "He was a good man," he said. "He provided for us, protected us, and loved deeply." The crowd wept. They couldn't understand how a man who seemed so strong could carry so much pain.

His brother continued, his voice trembling yet firm, "Talk to your family. Talk to your friends. Don't hide your struggles. Get help, see a therapist, share what's heavy on your heart. Don't keep your secrets locked away. Unmask your pain. Share, live, and love." The words lingered in the room, wrapping around every grieving soul like a quiet call to healing. Jonathan's coworkers came dressed in white with touches of gold, symbolizing the brightness of his career and the achievements he had made. The gentle shimmer of gold reflected the light of candles, reminding everyone of how brightly his spirit had once shone. His manager stood at the front and softly sang "Amazing Grace," her voice breaking at every verse, yet filled with gratitude for the life he lived.

The entertainment industry mourned his loss, but his legacy lived on. Those who knew him personally spoke of his kindness, humility, and the quiet pain he carried behind his smile. His films, interviews, and stories continued to inspire others to speak up about mental health. Even in death, Jonathan's life carried a purpose far beyond fame or applause; it became a story of courage, healing, and faith. Through his life and his pain, people learned that being strong doesn't mean hiding your hurt. His story touched hearts and opened eyes, reminding the world that every smile hides something deeper: joy, sorrow, or lessons that shape who we are. Jonathan's life showed that even after loss, love and purpose can still shine. Behind every smile, there is a story, and sometimes, a second face.

Chapter 3

The Woman behind the Mask

The woman behind the mask. Who is she? Does she even know? What does she want out of life? Why is she hiding? What is she reaching for? What is she afraid to face?

These are the questions asked by the woman who wears the mask. She smiles on the outside, but inside, she is searching. She is searching for meaning, searching for direction, searching for the courage to be who she truly is.

She asks herself quietly: "If I ever take this mask off, will I still be enough?"

And that woman was Ms. Tiara Blake. Ms. Tiara Blake was a successful fashion designer living in downtown Chicago. Her passion for fashion was unmatched. She created masterpieces for celebrities, styled actors, singers, and anyone who needed to shine. In the industry, her name carried weight. People trusted her vision. They trusted her taste. They trusted her touch.

But Tiara, the woman behind the talent, was a mystery even to herself. She was a very plain woman with very big ideas. Her beauty was quiet and unannounced. She wore long, beautiful, wavy black hair that flowed gently down her back, yet she never styled it in ways that drew attention. She did not see the natural beauty she possessed, and she hid what made her truly striking.

She loved making everyone else around her look beautiful. She could transform others with ease, pulling elegance out of thin air. But when it came to her own self, she did not care. Her closet told the silent truth. As far as the eye could see, everything was black and white. Row after row of safe colors. Predictable and controlled. And in a few tucked-away spaces, a quiet navy blue. Those were the only shades she allowed herself to wear for industry events. Tiara poured beauty into others, yet hid her own. She knew how to dress the world, but she did not know how to dress herself. Because choosing those colors was not about fashion, it was about hiding.

One cold day in Chicago, the wind was whipping off Lake Michigan, pushing toward zero-degree weather. Tiara glanced at her reflection as she headed into her office building. Tears filled her eyes as she thought about her life. She thought kindly about her parents, who had moved away years ago. They wanted to leave the big city and enjoy a quiet, remote life in the country.

By that time, Tiara was already successful. She still talked to them, but not enough. She felt the distance, not only in miles but emotionally. As she reflected, she noticed that Mother Time had played her part in her life. The woman she was looking at no longer resembled the little girl she once knew.

Tiara whispered to herself: "Who am I?"

That question followed her like a shadow. As she walked down the banks of her memory, she remembered how she used to draw on the ground whenever an idea came to her. Whenever a design hit her mind, she had to get it out. She remembered how she would even draw on the walls when she forgot her drawing pad. And she remembered the punishment she received for doing it. But those punishments taught her something important. They taught her to never leave home without her drawing pad again.

Her mind drifted to her high school years. She remembered how she first gained the attention of the fashion industry. She remembered slipping into a bathroom stall one afternoon, unable to hold an idea any longer. She forgot her drawing pad again, so she drew her design on the bathroom wall. That same drawing was discovered by someone who recognized raw talent. That same drawing led to her work being featured in Essence magazine, worn by the world-renowned Gabrielle Union.

From that moment, her career skyrocketed. After high school, she went to the University of Creative Mind, and she excelled there. Her professors saw her brilliance. Her classmates saw her passion.

Everyone saw her potential rising right before their eyes. Everyone saw her, except for her.

Because even in her success, she was still the woman behind the mask. Tiara never made time for her personal life. She was very goal-oriented when it came to her skillful talent. Her work was always first. She never made time to have fun or take vacations. The only time she would travel was when it was work-related. Everything in her life had a purpose, and that purpose was tied to her career.

As she continued to reflect, she remembered a man who once showed interest in her. He would leave flowers for her and little notes expressing how he felt.

Sometimes she would find a card or a thoughtful message tucked into her mailbox. But she never entertained him at all. She never allowed herself to receive the love he was trying to give. Eventually, he stopped trying to pursue her. She did not blame him. She knew she had shut the door before he ever had a chance to knock. A time or two, Tiara went home to visit her now-aged parents, who missed her more than she ever realized. When she visited, they would hug her with tears running down their faces, reminding her of how much they loved her. They did not understand what had caused the distance. They never judged her or questioned her behavior. They simply showed her the love she so desperately needed, even if she did not know how to accept it.

Her mind continued to wander down memory lane as she thought about her birthday coming in a few weeks. She whispered to herself:

"I am going to be 35, and I have no husband and no children."

She remembered how she always wanted at least five children because she grew up as an only child and felt so alone. Then she thought within herself:

"I have to do better. I need to stop hiding. I need to stop hiding behind this mask of fear and unworthiness."

While walking back to the office, Tiara called one of her best friends, someone she had kept in touch with throughout the years. It was her college roommate, Ashley. Ashley had become a successful teacher. She taught first graders and loved it. She always had a heart for children and family. She was married now, eight years strong, with two beautiful boys.

Ashley was easy to talk to. She listened as Tiara poured out what had been weighing on her heart. Tiara told her everything that had been plaguing her mind.

Ashley said gently, "I am so glad you are talking about this. You know, we have talked about this from time to time again. It is good for you to get these feelings out because you are worthy of love. You are worthy of being loved, Tiara. I have been praying for you, even this morning, and I know it was God who put me on your mind to call."

Ashley continued to encourage her and prayed for her until Tiara started to feel a little better. When they finally hung up, Tiara sat there holding her phone, realizing that something inside her had shifted. She knew her life would be different after the conversation with her friend.

She whispered to herself: "What should I do?"

Before she could finish the thought, she felt a gentle stirring in her spirit. A voice she had not heard in a long time. A voice she recognized instantly.

Jesus spoke to her heart, saying: "Come unto me, all you who are weary and burdened, and I will give you rest."

Tiara fell down on her knees and said, "Yes, Lord, I hear you. I cannot do this on my own."

She wept. After she had this beautiful encounter with the Lord, she made up in her heart that it was time to let go and let God. A calmness settled over her spirit, the kind she had not felt in years. She knew this moment was the beginning of a new chapter in her life.

Chapter 4

Tiara's Awakening

As Tiara gazed into her antique brass mirror in the bathroom, she noticed a glow on her face that only could be given by God. She felt a sense of peace in her life. She couldn't explain it, but she knew it was the joy of the Lord. As she continued to get dressed, she noticed how beautiful the weather was outside. It was a gorgeous Sunday morning. The air was fresh and clean. It reminded her of the days when she was a child.

She wore a beautiful purple dress with ruffled sleeves and pleats that moved whenever she did. She thought to herself, "It's been a long time since I've been in the house of the Lord. I'm a bit nervous, but I'm going anyway."

As she parked her gray BMW, she felt as if God had set His approval on what she was doing. She paused for a moment, letting the engine settle, and breathed in the stillness around her. When she looked toward the east, she saw three beautiful, colorful eagles soaring in the sky. Their wings stretched wide, gliding effortlessly as if carried by the very breath of God. The colors on their feathers shimmered in the sunlight, hues she had never seen on an eagle before. It felt like a sign, a quiet reminder that heaven was watching over her steps.

A warm feeling rushed through her chest. She whispered, "Lord, thank You for guiding me today."

Tiara couldn't get her phone out fast enough to capture the moment. Her hands trembled with excitement, but the eagles were gone before she could snap a picture. Still, the image stayed in her heart.

The first thing she saw when she entered the lovely sanctuary was a group of children in their yellow choir robes getting ready to sing. Their little voices floated in warm chatter as they lined up, full of joy and innocence.

She noticed a beautiful decoration on the side of the altar. It was two golden seraphims, their wings lifted high, and between them they held a sign that read: "Holy, Holy, Holy is the Lord of Hosts."

The children began to sing a song she had never heard before. The words went like this: "I trust in God, my Savior, the One who will never fail."

Another verse said: "I sought the Lord, and He heard me, and He answered. That's why I trust Him."

As she listened to the words of the song, tears flooded her face as she worshipped the Lord. The purity in their voices reached places in her heart she didn't even realize were still tender. She let the tears fall freely. It felt like healing.

After the choir finished singing, someone brought Tiara a tissue to wipe her lovely eyes. As she dabbed her tears, she noticed a face that seemed familiar. It was the face of the man who had tried to reach out to her before, the one who had tried to show her the love she so desperately needed. He was watching her in the service, and she knew it, but she continued to praise God.

The preacher stepped forward, preparing to preach. "May I have your attention, please?" he said. "Let us turn to the book of Matthew, chapter 11, verse 28."

He read with power: "Come unto me, all ye who are weary and burdened, and I will give you rest."

And the whole church responded, "Amen."

The preacher continued, speaking about the love of God, loving yourself first, and then loving others. He reminded the congregation that only what we do for Christ is going to last. Tiara held on to every word, applying them to her life as she let God heal her.

Then he said, "God sees you, and He is calling for you. Come… come to Jesus."

Before she realized it, Tiara instantly got up with both hands lifted high, as if something beyond her own strength was moving her. She walked toward the altar with trembling steps, then kneeled down and fell under the power of God. She was filled with the presence of the Holy Spirit. It was a feeling she had never felt before, a feeling that made her new, a feeling that made her free.

After that beautiful anointed service, different ones in the congregation came up and hugged Tiara. Even people from her job recognized her. They were so happy for her as they embraced her warmly.

Finally, the man who had pursued her approached. His smile was gentle. "It is so good to see you here, Tiara," he said.

She smiled back. "Thank you. It's good to be here."

They embraced and then walked out the door together.

Still feeling wonderful from the service, Tiara spoke with Siri and had her call her mother and father. With excitement in her voice, she said, "Mother, I went to church today. The Lord did exactly what I was looking for. He saved me."

Her parents were so happy that tears began to flow down their faces. She could tell they were crying even through the phone. She remembered the words of her father when he said, "Now, you should be able to see clearly."

She pondered those words in her heart as she hung up the phone. Then she called her friend Ashley. With that same energy and joy, she told her what she had done and what she had experienced. Ashley was overwhelmed with happiness for her.

Everybody was very happy for Tiara. They all knew she was entering a new season of her life, one filled with purpose, peace, and the presence of God. She had always been successful, but now her life would be complete, because she finally had Jesus as the center of her joy.

Chapter 5

The New Me

A brand new day was at hand as Tiara looked through that same brass mirror in her bathroom. She looked at herself and said, "I can write a book about my life."

She thought to herself, I will call it The New Me. She smiled and continued to put on a little makeup and lip-gloss as she got ready for work.

Tiara parked her BMW and made her way toward her office. She always had to pass the glass doors that showed her reflection. In anticipation of that moment, she walked slowly. Looking into the glass that reflected her image, she saw a woman who was new, a woman who was revived. Restored. Alive.

Tiara had a little color in her face because the joy of the Lord was all over her. She saw herself as beautiful as she continued walking and entered the doors. When she stepped into the building, she turned heads. Her team, her co-workers, were looking like: "Who is that lady?"

And she wore a smile that said everything her spirit already knew.

Her co-workers were wondering what in the world had happened to her.

She had color on now. She no longer wore the black and white she used to hide behind. Her hair was pinned up in a style that showed her full face. She looked great. She wore a gold blazer with cream pants and a little stylish heel that shone.

She said to everybody: "Good morning, everyone."

Her voice carried the confidence she now possessed. The mask had been replaced with a beautiful smile.

Before she opened up her computer, Tiara spoke softly to the Lord. She whispered: "I will praise Thee, for I am fearfully and wonderfully made.

Marvelous are Thy works, and that my soul knoweth right well. Thank You, Lord, for loving me when I didn't even love myself. Thank You for giving me rest and allowing me to come unto You. I was weary and burdened… now my soul is resting, thanking You for the goodness of God."

Tiara went on to live a beautiful life. The Lord blessed her with a nice husband who loved her, the same gentleman who never gave up on her. His name was Larry. He told her, "I loved you since the first day I saw you."

She finally started to love herself, so she could accept love. They were married, had three beautiful children, and she lived a full life surrounded by friends, family, and co-workers she helped along the way. God had been good to her.

Tiara wrote that book she had talked about, The New Me, and it told all the things she had hidden from the world. She wrote about the mask she had worn for so long and how God changed the way she looked at herself. She wrote how she could finally take the mask off.

She said, "Now I want you all to read my story and learn that you don't have to hide. God will help you put on the smile, the face He intended for you to have. My book, The New Me.

May you be blessed.

May you show your true self.

May you reflect the very image of Christ. Amen."

Chapter 6

The Face Is Exposed

Hope was raised on a farm in Mississippi. Hope was a very beautiful, chocolate-skinned girl. She stood about 5 feet 8 inches tall and weighed approximately 110 pounds. Her complexion glowed, but Hope never realized how beautiful she was. She would get up early to help her grandma feed the chickens and the other farm animals. She never liked doing it, but she did it anyway because she was told. One day, Hope got ready to feed the pigs. She carried the corn up to the trough, and as she poured it in, another pig came charging toward her. She fell into the mud, furious and frightened.

Hope never liked getting dirty. She was covered with mud from head to toe. She ran back into the house, screaming, "Grandma!" After she showered and cleaned up, she sat on the couch to watch television. Grandma came in and said, "Are you okay, girl?" Hope said, "Yes, ma'am. But when I get grown, I'm moving to New York City. I'm never going to live this type of life." Grandma said, "This life is not so bad, baby." Hope said, "Well, I don't like it." Grandma laughed until tears rolled down her face. Hope didn't think it was funny, so she ran out of the room. She went to the bathroom, looked in the mirror, and saw herself still speckled with mud.

As soon as she could, she quickly took off her clothes and carefully cleaned herself again, feeling overwhelmed and upset. Grandma reassured her that she didn't need to go back outside, so Hope decided to stay indoors and enjoy her books. Later, Hope shyly asked, "Grandma, is it okay if I go downtown?" Grandma smiled kindly and responded, "Of course, sweetheart. What do you have in mind today?" Hope explained, "Oh, just to look at the store windows. I've got a little bit of money." Grandma nodded warmly, saying, "Alright, my dear, just be careful out there."

After spending her money browsing the shops, Hope headed back home. As she walked along, she suddenly noticed a man following her. Feeling uneasy, she picked up her pace and then broke into a run. The streets were quiet and empty. Before she knew it, he caught up with her, pulled her behind some bushes, and touched her in ways no one ever should. Hope, only thirteen, ran home crying, overwhelmed and scared. "Grandma, someone hurt me!" she cried out. Grandma immediately asked, "Who did this?" Hope, trembling, replied, "I don't know. He was a white, skinny man." Grandma gently suggested, "We need to call the police right away." Fearful he might return, Hope begged her to stay silent, worried about what might happen next.

That night, Grandma fixed Hope's favorite dinner, fried chicken, mashed potatoes, and cornbread, but Hope couldn't eat. Grandma told her they needed to find out who had done this. Hope said quietly, "It was Uncle Charlie." Grandma gasped. "Don't be insane, girl. Your uncle would never do that to you." Hope insisted, "Grandma, it was him." Grandma said harshly, "Don't you ever say that again. Go to bed and don't come down until you apologize." Hope went to her room and cried all night. "Grandma doesn't believe me," she whispered. "It was him. I saw him." Lying in bed, she thought about her mother and wondered why she always had to stay with Grandma. "Why not with Mom? Why am I always here?"

The questions haunted her. The next morning, she apologized just to keep the peace, but inside, she was angry. She told herself, "This is not what love looks like. You're supposed to believe a child." From that moment, she promised she would leave that place and never come back. Years passed. Holidays and family gatherings came and went. Hope stayed distant, isolating herself. One Fourth of July, the family reunion was held at Grandma's house. Hope stayed in her room reading, refusing to go out. After the reunion, Grandma came to check on her, kissed her forehead, and left quietly.

As summer ended, Hope prepared for her senior year. She had grown taller and looked like a model. One Saturday, Grandma and Hope went school-shopping. At the mall, Hope tripped into a young man named Joseph. "I'm so sorry," he said. "Please forgive me." Hope was embarrassed. Joseph was struck by her beauty.

Later, after shopping, Hope and Grandma returned home, and there stood Joseph outside the house. "How did he find out where we live?" Grandma asked. Hope didn't know but secretly felt curious. Joseph said, "I hope I'm not being impulsive, but I couldn't stop thinking about you." He asked for her number. She told him she didn't have a phone. Grandma said, "You can give him the house number." Hope replied shyly, "I'll think about it." He asked if he could see her tomorrow. "Maybe," she said. "Around twelve," he added. She nodded.

The next day, Hope got dressed, pretending not to be excited, but she was. Joseph arrived and greeted Grandma politely before taking a seat on the couch. When Hope walked in, he smiled warmly. They exchanged greetings and stepped outside to sit on the porch. For hours, they talked, sipping soda and sharing sandwiches.

When school started again, Hope was thrilled. She and Joseph grew close, often doing homework together and spending time at the mall. With him, she felt safe. Joseph usually walked her home after school. One afternoon, she asked, "How tall are you?"

"About six-four," he said. "Wow," she smiled. "You're tall."

He laughed softly. "You're beautiful."

Hope looked down, blushing. At her door, he asked, "Can I get a kiss?"

"No," she replied, then quickly kissed his cheek before hurrying inside, grinning from ear to ear.

One evening, Grandma cooked fried chicken, black-eyed peas, cornbread, and lemon cake. "Hope," she said, "I'm so happy for you and Joseph. You two are so cute together."

Hope smiled. "He's nice, Grandma, but I'm scared. I don't know much about relationships."

Grandma nodded. "You'll learn. And if you ever have problems, come to me. He sounds like a good one."

Hope said, "I think he wants to ask me to the prom."

Grandma's eyes lit up. "That's wonderful! We'll get you a beautiful dress."

When prom season arrived, Hope was ecstatic. "It's tonight!" she told Grandma, her voice sparkling with excitement. The school was buzzing with excitement as classes ended early, giving students a chance to get ready. Hope spent the afternoon getting her hair and makeup done, then waited at home in her beautiful dress. Joseph arrived in a sharp black tuxedo with a purple bow tie, while Hope wore a stunning purple gown adorned with tiny pearls. Together, they looked like a picture-perfect couple.

At prom, they enjoyed sweet punch, laughter, and countless smiles. When the song *"I Will Always Love You"* began to play,

Joseph gently asked, "Do you want to dance?" Hope hesitated. "I don't know how," she admitted. Smiling, Joseph assured her, "Just follow my lead." As they danced, the world around them seemed to fade, their movements soft and graceful, lost in the rhythm of the song.

Later that evening, Joseph asked softly, "Are you ready to head home? It's already getting late." Hope nodded. "Yes." He smiled. "Want to go for a little ride?" She agreed happily, and the two talked and held hands as the limo glided through the quiet city streets. When he walked her to her door, they shared a sweet, tender kiss. "Goodnight, I love you," he whispered. "I love you too," she replied softly.

Graduation day arrived like a bright sunrise of new beginnings. Grandma gently asked, "What am I going to do without you, girl?" Hope comforted her with a warm smile. "You'll be just fine, Grandma. I've always dreamed of moving to New York someday." Grandma looked curious. "What about Joseph?" Hope beamed proudly. "He's heading to Howard in D.C., so we'll be only a few hours apart."

That night, Hope lay in bed feeling at peace, yet her thoughts drifted back to a shadow from the past, Uncle Charlie. She and Grandma were on good terms now, but part of her still ached that Grandma hadn't believed her. Years later, when Hope finally reunited with her family, she found the courage to speak the truth that had long haunted her. Though Uncle Charlie had passed away, saying his name out loud finally released the pain. She felt lighter than ever before, free to live, love, and breathe without shame.

Hope's healing journey inspired her to start a mentoring program after sharing her story with her family. The program brought together young girls who had faced painful experiences, offering them a safe, understanding space to talk, connect, and heal. This became her joy and purpose: to give others the support she never had when she needed it most. She wanted the next generation to feel safe, so she founded *The House of Exposure*, a place where young women could open up, find trust, and let God meet them where they were.

It became a refuge of strength, compassion, and faith, a sanctuary of release, healing, and hope.

Chapter 7

A Face of Hope

After a long day at school, Hope was very tired, but she knew she had to stop by The House of Exposure. She was deeply committed to her mission, and the girls depended on her. They talked about everything. Hope shared her own story, offering light and understanding about what had happened to her years ago. She reminded the girls that they were safe, and they believed her. They loved Hope and the supportive team she had built. Hope had a powerful influence on the girls and everyone in her community.

Graceful and a little old-fashioned, Hope carried herself with quiet confidence. She was respected by her colleagues and adored by Joseph. One evening, Hope said softly, "Yes, Joseph, yes. I love you." Time seemed to stand still as the two sat together after all the excitement. Joseph reached for Hope's hand and quoted Scripture 1 Corinthians 15:19:

"If in this life only we have hope in Christ, we are of all men most miserable."

He continued gently, "Like Paul was saying in the scripture, without Christ we wouldn't have any hope, and we'd be miserable. Without you, Hope, I would be miserable. I love you. I'm so blessed to be able to call you mine."

Hope looked at him in amazement. "When did you get so spiritual?"

Joseph smiled. "I've been attending services in D.C. sometimes. I felt I needed something more, something was missing. I had the opportunity to go to a small church and realized I needed salvation. I didn't get the chance to tell you until now."

Tears welled in Hope's eyes. "Joseph, you are a gift," she said. "You've helped me in so many ways." As she spoke, her mind drifted to her dark past and how Joseph had filled the emptiness she once felt. He squeezed her hand gently and kissed her. "You can trust me," he whispered.

Feeling safe, Hope began to open up about her past. For the first time, she spoke freely about her mother giving her away and letting Grandma raise her. She talked about the painful incident with Uncle Charlie and how she had missed growing up with her siblings. It all poured out of her. But Joseph already knew. He had never brought it up, never pushed.

Curious yet compassionate, Joseph listened carefully and asked gentle questions. Then he said, "It's all good. I love you. You mean everything to me."

Hope smiled through her tears. "You know," she said softly, "you're the first man I've ever let into my life and get this close to me."

"I'm so happy I tripped into you that day at the mall," Hope said, and they both smiled and hugged. Joseph held her close and whispered, "I love you, and you're safe. No one will ever hurt you again."

The couple was so in love. After sharing their deepest hurts and fears, they sat on the couch, sipping tea and watching *The Notebook*. It was one of Hope's favorite movies; she was always a hopeless romantic. Joseph looked at her and said, "That's going to be us one day." She smiled and replied, "Yes, I don't ever want to forget you." They both smiled and cuddled, sharing a compassionate kiss.

The very next morning, Joseph was at Hope's door.

His heart pounded. He barely had time to think; he just knew he couldn't wait any longer. The moment she opened the door, he spoke.

"Hope," he said, breathless, "I wanted to ask you last night, but I didn't have the nerve. I love you. You know that. I've loved you since the first moment I saw you. You're the reason my heart beats."

He pulled a small box from his pocket, opened it with shaking hands, and dropped to one knee.

"I don't want to wait another minute. Please, make me the happiest man in the world. Will you marry me?"

Hope's face froze. Her eyes widened, her lips parted, and then tears welled up in her eyes.

"Yes, Joseph. I will marry you," she whispered. "I love you more than you'll ever know."

He stood and scooped her into his arms, spinning her in three joyful circles.

"I'm gonna give you the world," he said, laughing. "I can't wait to tell Grandma."

"We'll call her three-way," Hope said. "Sounds good. Let's do it."

Hope could hardly sit still. Her heart was racing faster than her thoughts. She was glowing giddy. The day couldn't pass fast enough. She kept staring at the ring on her finger, solid and shining, proof that what she had dreamed about her whole life was finally happening.

She thought of all the wedding stories she read as a little girl, imagining herself in the pages. Today, those pages had turned real.

A tear slipped down her cheek. She whispered, "Thank you. Thank you, God, for every trial, every test, everything I've been through. You didn't forget about me. You gave me the desire of my heart. I'm grateful."

Later that day, they called Grandma.

She answered just as she sat down on the couch with a warm bowl of soup and a mug of hot tea.

"Hello?"

"Hi, Grandma!" Hope said, practically glowing through the phone. "Joseph's on the line too."

"Hi, Joseph," she said warmly. "How are you doing, dear?" "I couldn't be happier," he said. "We have some news." "Oh?" Grandma perked up. "What's going on?"

"Don't worry, it's good news," he said with a smile in his voice. "Grandma, you know how much I love Hope. I've already asked her to marry me, and she said yes. But I wanted to tell you myself. I want your blessing, too. It means everything to us."

There was a beat of silence, then Grandma's voice came, thick with emotion.

"Oh, Joseph... I knew this day would come. You've always been like a son to me. Of course, you have my blessing. I'm so happy for you both. God bless you."

"Thank you, Grandma," they said together. "We love you," Hope added, her voice soft.

"I love you too. I'll let the rest of the family know."
"Thank you so much," Hope said.

"Thank you for loving each other," Grandma replied. "Now go enjoy this moment. It's yours."

But even through the celebration, a quiet ache lingered in Hope's heart, a missing piece.

Later that evening, she called Grandma again. Her voice was different, softer, more reflective.

"Grandma," she said gently, "I'm really happy. Everything feels like it's finally coming together. I know I'm blessed."

There was a pause.

"But I also know there's something I need to face. I need to make things right with Mom. I need to forgive her."

Grandma didn't speak. She just listened.

"I can't move into this next chapter of my life carrying old pain. I want peace. And I want her to be part of this. This is the happiest time of my life, and I want to share it with her fully. With a clean heart."

Her voice broke just a little, but she didn't cry. She just breathed. "I think it's time."

So Grandma gave her the number, and Hope called her mother. The two reconnected, sharing memories, updates, and long-missed laughter. Hope told her mom about the wedding, how happy she was, and how much she wanted to rebuild their relationship.

Later, Hope reflected on her journey and realized that every trial had shaped her into the woman she had become. She was thankful for every heartache, every sleepless night, every missed meal, and every family gathering she couldn't attend. Each hardship had led her closer to God's purpose. She smiled and whispered a prayer of gratitude, knowing it was all worth it because God had truly smiled on her. Her mother had named her Hope for a reason. Though her mother hadn't known the meaning behind the name at the time, God did. It was the perfect name, because without hope, life would indeed be miserable.

Hope and Joseph built a beautiful life together. They raised their children with strong faith, teaching them the love of God, the importance of family, and the power of prayer. They reminded their children to love, respect, and communicate with one another, and to never lose faith.

The House of Exposure continued to thrive as a community cornerstone run by Hope and Joseph with a dedicated staff. It flourished and became well-known in the city and surrounding areas, a beacon of healing and strength. This story reminds us always to wear the face of hope. No matter what challenges life brings, there is always hope. And we can rest assured that if God is for us, no one can stand against us.

Like Hope, God always intended to take care of her, just as He takes care of all of us. So live your best life. Let God fulfill every need and desire within His plan. In this life, you'll find peace, and in the next, joy that surpasses understanding. Together, the couple continued to study the Word of God. They grew spiritually strong, becoming a true power couple grounded in faith. They learned and showed themselves approved unto God, a workman who needed not to be ashamed, rightly dividing the Word of Truth.

Hope's favorite scripture was 1 Corinthians 2:9:

"But as it is written, Eye hath not seen, nor ear heard, neither have entered into the heart of man, the things which God hath prepared for them that love him."

Chapter 8

The Face of Truth

On Lincoln Street in New York City, a beautiful spring morning unfolded in the spring of 2022. The weather was refreshing and alive after a long, harsh, icy winter. The air felt crisp and clean, a perfect setup for a bright, colorful day.

After her morning devotions and quiet time with God, Hope poured herself a big cup of coffee, her cherished morning ritual before leaving for her daily assignment. As she sipped, her thoughts drifted back over her life. For a brief moment, she reflected on the deep sense of fulfillment she felt through every mentee she had helped, and how each story became a doorway to change.

The House of Exposure had become her defining mission, and she was grateful to share that purpose with Joseph. Together, they extended support to a world yearning for healing.

Hope frequently told her students that suppressing pain can harm you physically, mentally, and spiritually. That's why The House of Exposure was vital, it was a secure environment for healing and renewal.

Later that day, Hope was teaching and sharing with a group of new mentees when one of the young women stood up and said softly, "I have something to share."

Hope smiled gently and said, "You don't have to stand, sweetheart. Sit down, babe."

The new mentee sat down, her voice trembling. "I've been here for two weeks," she said, "and I wasn't able to open up, but now it's time. I want to share."

She took a deep breath. "One morning, I was sitting in my classroom studying when my teacher came over and whispered something in my ear. It was very inappropriate. This is the first time I've spoken about it. What should I do?"

Hope said softly, "Do you care to share what he said?"

The girl nodded. "Yes, ma'am. My teacher's name is Mr. Maldi, and he said, 'I know a good way you can earn an A, beautiful.' I looked up at him with disgust in my eyes, and he backed away. I walked out of the classroom crying. I haven't told anyone until now."

Without hesitation, Hope went to her and wrapped her arms around the young girl. "I'm so glad you opened up about this," she said gently. "The first thing we need to do is tell your parents.

After that, let them handle it, and we'll be here to support you."

The mentee nodded, tears streaming down her thin, fair face. "It's only my mom," she whispered. "My father died three years ago. He had cancer. My mom's still trying to get by, so I thought I should start here. That's why I came to share."

Hope held her tighter. "We'll take care of it," she assured her. "Everything's going to be all right. Don't you worry about a thing. We'll make sure this is handled with care, discretion, and professionalism."

About that time, there was a knock at the door. All the mentees looked around curiously. Hope walked over to see who it was and to her surprise, it was her mother.

Hope was taken by surprise, not only because it was unexpected, but also because it was against the rules to interrupt a session.

Still, seeing her mother there, she smiled and said gently, "Mom, can you give me just a few minutes until the session is finished?"

Her mother nodded. "Sure, I'll wait outside until you're ready. Thank you."

Hope turned back to the group and wrapped up the session. She reassured the girls that they were safe, supported, and in the right place at the right time to share their stories. To the mentee who had spoken earlier about her teacher, Hope added that they would handle the situation very soon and with care.

When the mentees entered the refreshment room, Hope gently stepped into the hallway to find her mother and kindly guided her into the office. As they moved, Hope instinctively noticed a worried, almost frightened look in her mother's eyes, as if she had something important to share but was struggling to find the right words.

While waiting in the hall, her mother caught sight of Joseph across the room. She hesitated, unsure whether to speak, but Joseph noticed her first.

"Hey," he said warmly. "Hello," she replied.

"How's Miss Lydia doing, my beautiful mother-in-law?" he asked with a grin. Then he gave her a big hug and kissed her on the cheek.

"I'm doing well," she said softly. "What brings you here today?"

"Oh," she replied, "I need to talk to my daughter."

"Okay," he said, smiling. "It's good to see you."

"It's good to see you too," she answered.

Once inside the office, Ms. Lydia took a deep breath. "Hope, I know we talk quite often," she began, "but I wanted to speak to you in person. I have something to get off my chest, something that's been tugging at me for a long time. I thought it was time to tell you what's really in my heart."

She hesitated, her voice trembling. "I follow you on social media, and I see how good and how successful the House of Exposure has become. I've listened to some of the children's stories; they speak so highly of you and Joseph. It made me realize that being open, honest, and caring about each other's feelings is what truly heals. I wanted to tell you this long ago, but I couldn't. It was too hard. I didn't have the strength to face it. But now... the Lord has pricked my heart to be open to finally tell the truth."

Tears filled Hope's eyes. "What is it, Mom? It's okay," she whispered.

Her mother's voice broke as she spoke. "Hope, I've always believed what you said about Uncle Charlie," she said. "He started touching me in places I didn't want him to touch. I told him no, told him to stop, that I would tell someone. But anytime we were alone, and I tried my best to avoid those moments, it happened again. Then one day, he touched me, and I began screaming, 'I'm going to tell! I'm going to tell!' He didn't care. He put his hand over my mouth... and he did the unthinkable."

"As a result of that night, I became pregnant," Lydia said softly.

"I had never felt so hurt, so broken, and so violated in my entire life. I cried many nights, wanting to tell someone what had happened to me, but I just didn't have the courage."

Months passed, three, maybe four, and I started to notice my body changing. My stomach was growing larger, and things just felt off.

I knew something was wrong. Finally, I confided in one of my girlfriends at school. She looked at me and said, 'Girl, you look pregnant.'

"I said, 'No way,' and I started crying. Deep down, I already knew if I was pregnant, I knew who the father was, and it tore me apart inside. I kept that secret for as long as I could, but eventually, it became impossible to hide. My mom took me to the doctor. When the doctor said I was five months pregnant, she was floored.

"She was so upset. She said, 'What, girl? You know better than this. What's going on with you? You know what we taught you: waiting until marriage is important. You're supposed to wait until you have a husband.'

"I tried to explain. I said, 'But Mom,' and she cut me off. 'Don't "but Mom" me.'

That was the moment I gently told her, 'Mom, I need to share what truly happened to me.' I reminded her kindly that I'd mentioned several times before that Uncle Charlie had hurt me in ways he shouldn't have, but she hadn't believed me. Then I opened up completely: about the day he cornered me, touched me, and did the unthinkable.

"Grandma didn't believe me either. She swore to this day that it couldn't have happened. So I left, Hope. I went to your auntie's house. I told her everything. She listened and believed me. She said, 'Do you want me to tell your mother?' I said, 'Yes.' She did, but even then, your mother never believed it."

Lydia paused, her voice trembling as tears streamed down her face. "And that's how I ended up giving birth to you, Hope. Uncle Charlie is your father."

The words hit Hope like a wave. Her heart pounded, and tears flooded her eyes. She couldn't speak. Without a word, she stood up and ran out of the room to find her husband.

When she found Joseph, she gasped, "Joseph, you won't believe what I just heard." Between sobs, she told him everything her mother had said.

Joseph wrapped his arms around her. "Let's pray," he said quietly. He held her close and began to pray aloud:

"Father, in the name of Jesus, touch my wife right now. Touch her where the pain hurts the most. From the crown of her head to the soles of her feet, heal her inside and out. Lord, lay Your hands on this dear woman I love so deeply, my beloved, my Hope, the reason I even know You today. Touch her, Lord. And while you touch her, touch her mother too. Thank you for giving her the courage to speak the truth. Comfort her, God, even in this moment. We know You are King of Kings and Lord of Lords. There's nothing hidden from You. Do what you do best, God."

Joseph continued praying until the Spirit of the Lord filled the room. As he prayed, Miss Lydia overheard his voice and began to weep. She walked in quietly, took both Joseph's and Hope's hands, and joined them in prayer.

And the Lord intervened exactly where they needed Him most. That day, God showed them that being united in honesty and openness mattered more than anything else, and with His support, they could face whatever challenges life presented.

He also impressed upon their hearts the importance of forgiveness. They had to forgive Uncle Charlie. Though he had already passed on, forgiveness was still necessary. The same was true for Grandma, Miss Lydia's mother. She, too, needed to be forgiven, not because she was right, but because deep down, she only wanted to believe it hadn't happened. Yet, in her heart, she knew it was true.

So they prayed together, saying:

"Lord, we thank You for bringing us together and for opening this avenue so that truth could be revealed. We thank You for loving us enough to let us face the truth, because You said that the truth shall set us free. And we thank You, in Jesus' name. Amen."

From that day forward, God changed the way Hope and her mother felt toward each other. He drew them closer than ever, leaving no more secrets or distance between them. The family continued to grow stronger, united in love and rooted in prayer.

The Bible reminds us that we should always pray and not give up. Prayer is vital to the Christian life. It brings us closer to God and helps us share the deepest parts of our hearts with Him. Even though He already knows us inside and out, prayer allows us to approach Him openly and sincerely. When we do, He heals us and fills us with a peace that surpasses understanding. Because God is love, we learn how to love one another. Because God is love, we learn how to care for one another in spirit and in truth. We are children of the light; therefore, we take no part in darkness. Instead, we bring light into dark places so that the world can see Jesus in us.

This should be our daily prayer:

"Lord, let someone see Jesus in me. Not my will, dear Father, but Yours be done. Show them that you are the way, the truth, and the life. Your light cannot be hidden; it shines through the darkest and the lowest places of our hearts and minds, a city set on a hill that cannot be hidden. We are the salt of the earth." And God, we thank You for loving us enough to let us encourage someone, to let us witness to someone, and to fulfill the work You have given us. As You said, 'Go ye into the highways and hedges and compel them to come in,' that Your house may be filled, that their spiritual house may be filled, so they can live in a way that pleases You. We thank You, Lord, and we love You with the love of Christ. Let us always walk in truth. Let our faith shine through everything we do. In Jesus' name, Amen."

Chapter 9

The Face of Mercy

After a heartfelt, sacred Sunday morning service, the next day, Ms. Lydia was preparing dinner for her family. She had been in communion with the Lord and attuned to His guidance. He told her to call her mother, Joseph, and Hope for an evening meal the following day. Lydia had become very faithful in her prayer life and was also receptive to what God was saying.

Lydia picked up the phone and called Hope. "Hope, can you and Joseph come over for dinner?"

"Yes, ma'am, that sounds wonderful," Hope said. "I'll make sure with Joseph, but you know how he is. He loves to eat."

"Grandma has already accepted the invitation," Lydia said. "I would love if you guys would come over. I'm making your favorite: fried chicken, cabbage, sweet potatoes, and cornbread."

"Yes, ma'am, that sounds wonderful," Hope said. "I'll make sure with Joseph, but I'm pretty sure it's fine."

In the back of both of their minds, they were thinking, *Oh Lord, why Monday? We had a long day at church yesterday.* But nevertheless, they agreed to go.

Joseph smiled and said, "Yes, I was thinking of catching a movie. We were going to chill with Netflix." They both chuckled.

Lydia and her mother talked from time to time, but Lydia wanted a closer relationship with her mama. She had been praying about it, and God gave her this vision of dinner. Lydia had learned not to question God, but she wondered, *Mother is the best cook in the world. I'm not sure how she'll enjoy my food, but nevertheless, I'll be obedient.*

Lydia could cook well. The kitchen smelled so good that the dogs outside were sniffing and barking, wanting to come in. Lydia was just taking the cornbread out of the oven when she began to talk to God.

"Dear Father, here I am again," she prayed. "I want you to bless this food, bless my family, bless my mama. I love her. I know we haven't always been at our best, but you know all things. I love her because she's the only mother I have. So I'm asking you, even now as I get this dinner ready, to be in the middle of everything we do. I know if you're in the middle, everything will be all right."

Suddenly, Lydia felt a calm wash over her heart, a peace she couldn't explain. She took a deep breath, wiping away the last trace of worry, and began to prepare the table. She placed a beautiful flower arrangement in the middle, the warm fall colors glowing softly in the afternoon light. Each petal seemed to reflect the peace she now carried inside. She carefully set the plates and silverware neatly, making sure everything was in its perfect place. The table looked absolutely gorgeous, filled with love, care, and the quiet joy of a woman whose spirit had finally found rest.

Lydia wanted to display the same mercy that Hope had given her, so she said softly, "Blessed are the merciful, for they shall obtain mercy." (Matthew 5:7) Then she whispered another, "Be ye therefore merciful, as your Father also is merciful." (Luke 6:36)

"Lord," she prayed, "thank You for these scriptures. I want to always remember Your love, kindness, mercy, and compassion toward us. That's what you desire for us to have, one toward another. I am willing, I am open, and I want to show love to my mom the same mercy You gave me. Thank You, Father."

The doorbell rang. Ms. Lydia hurried to open the door for her guest. To her surprise, Joseph was standing there holding a bouquet of red and cream roses so beautiful they seemed fake, but they were real.

"Thank you, son," Lydia said, hugging him. She placed the flowers in a vase she had tucked away in the closet. "You know what?" she said. "I'm going to put these on the table. They're prettier than what I had." And when she did, the table looked even more elegant. The atmosphere was set for a lovely evening.

"Can I get you anything to drink, or would you like an appetizer?" Lydia asked. "I have smoked meatballs and rotel dip as starters."

Joseph laughed. "You know me, I love to eat! I'll take some."

Hope smiled and asked, "Where's Grandma?" Lydia went to the kitchen while Hope tried to call her grandmother, but the phone kept ringing. She grew concerned, thinking maybe Grandma was on her way and didn't want to answer while driving.

Moments later, Hope's phone rang. It was the hospital. "Hello?" she said.

"Hope, this is the hospital," the voice said. "We tried calling Ms. Lydia, but you're listed as next of kin. Can you come to the hospital?"

"Is everything okay?" Hope asked.

"Just come. We'll explain everything here."

Hope hung up, told everyone what had happened, and before leaving, Joseph said, "Wait. Let's pray. We don't know what's up ahead, but prayer is always necessary." Joseph prayed, and they hurried to the emergency room.

When they arrived, the clerk checked and said, "Yes, follow

me." They walked to Ms. Martin's room, finding her asleep.

"Mom! Mom! How are you?" Lydia said.

Mrs. Martin opened her eyes slowly. "Where am I?"

"You're in the hospital, Mom," Hope said softly. "You must've driven here."

"Well," Mrs. Martin said, "I was supposed to be eating dinner with you all. What's going on?"

"It's okay, Mom," Hope said. "We're just glad you made it. The doctors are running tests."

As they talked, the doctor entered the room with a reassuring smile. "Everything looks good," he said kindly. "Your heart just needs some monitoring. We'll keep you here for a few hours, but you'll be able to head home soon and rest comfortably."

Mrs. Martin smiled with relief. "Maybe that's why that voice told me to go to the ER."

The doctor later returned and said, "She's fine to go home, but make sure she sees her family doctor soon for a heart checkup. Whatever made her come here, thank God for it."

The family took Mrs. Martin to Lydia's home. "Mom, you can rest on the couch if you're tired," Lydia said.

Mrs. Martin smiled. "No, baby. I want to sit at the table with you all and see your faces."

They helped her to the table, and Lydia said, "Mom, I've been praying."

Mrs. Martin said, "So have I. I love you, girl." They embraced tenderly.

Tears filled Lydia's eyes. "God has been dealing with me about mercy," she said. "I want us to have a relationship, Mom. We don't know when we'll leave here, but I forgive you, and I love you. I want to make things right."

Tears streamed down Mrs. Martin's face. "I'm sorry… I'm so sorry," she said, her voice trembling under the weight of years of silence. "I knew all along it was possible, Uncle Charlie did that to you both. It's hard even to say his name, but God has touched us.* He's softening our hearts and reminding us that forgiveness brings freedom. He wants us close again. He set this time and place for our healing. Thank you for showing me what it means to wear the face of mercy."*Mrs. Martin looked at her family and said, "Let us pray. Joseph, we know you love to pray. Will you lead us?"

Joseph bowed his head. "Father, thank You for this day," he prayed. "Thank You for Mother Martin. Thank You for letting her go to the emergency room, Lord. Anything could have happened, but Your grace and mercy were there by her side. Just like in

Psalm 23, You restore our souls. You've restored our family, our love, our hope, our mercy. Thank You for sending Your beloved Son Jesus to die for us. That was mercy, that was kindness, that was love. We thank You because You've healed this family. Bless this food in the name of Jesus. Take out anything that's not pleasing to You, purify it, sanctify it, and let it be nourishment to our bodies. In the mighty name of Jesus, Amen."

After dinner, Hope said, "I have some exciting news to share." Everyone looked around the table.

"What's going on, Hope?" Lydia asked.

Hope smiled softly and reached for Joseph's hand. "Joseph," she said, "you're going to be a father."

The room fell silent for a moment. Hope wasn't sure if this was the right place or the right moment to share, but she felt the Lord tugging at her heart. The Spirit said, Do it now, this is the moment, while love and mercy are in the air.

Joseph's eyes filled with tears as he stood up, walked over to Hope, and held her in his arms. "God is so good," he whispered. "In this same place where forgiveness and mercy met, He's blessing us with new life."

The family rejoiced. Laughter mixed with tears as the room filled with a warm sense of God's presence. Ms. Lydia wiped her eyes and said, "Look at God. When we walk in mercy, He rewards us with miracles." Her words carried a quiet power that touched every heart around the table. They laughed, cried, and prayed once more, grateful for the gift of love, the beauty of healing, and the lasting power of mercy, a mercy that would forever live on through their family and through generations to come.

Hope smiled, looking around the table. "Remember," she said softly, "Blessed are the merciful, for they shall obtain mercy." (Matthew 5:7)

God bless you.

Chapter 10

The Face of Blessing

On a cold winter day in December 2025, Hope and Joseph got ready to go to church as they normally do. Lydia stayed home that Sunday. She was planning a surprise gender reveal for Hope. So she called Hope's best friend, Susanna, to draw up the plan so they could surprise her after church.

Hope did not know her child's gender, but Joseph did. Hope preferred to be surprised and wanted to experience it the traditional way.

During the service, the preacher began to speak about the blessings of God. "The blessings of God are yea and amen," he said. "It's a divine favor. It's grace. And as a benefit, it's bestowed upon humanity, which includes a spiritual gift like forgiveness, adoption, eternal life, as well as material blessings."

He continued, "God offers forgiveness for sin through His Son, Jesus Christ, by grace. We are adopted into the royal family as daughters and sons of God. Blessings can bring comfort in times of mourning and suffering and grant peace in our souls. Blessings can involve protection and deliverance from trouble. Blessings are often described as being those who trust, seek, and delight in God."

The pastor had the congregation's full attention as they listened to him preach about the blessings of God. Some said, "Amen," others said, "Hallelujah," and most said, "Thank You, Jesus."

After the family enjoyed a beautiful service with the pastor and the congregation at church, they headed home. The message still echoed in their hearts as they drove, thankful for God's goodness. But before they went home, Hope wanted to stop and check on her grandmother, Ms. Martin. When she arrived, she smiled to see her grandmother sitting comfortably in her favorite chair, watching one of her beloved TV preachers with joy in her eyes.

Ms. Martin had already gone to her doctor earlier that week to get a referral to a cardiologist. They ran a full report, and the results were a blessing; everything looked healthy and strong. Her heart was fine. The doctor simply reminded her to take things slow, rest when she needed, and avoid worrying or overexerting herself. Hope thanked God quietly, grateful that her grandmother's heart, both physically and spiritually, was at peace.

He told her to take it easy, take a walk, and do a little exercise from her chair. "This is how you maintain a good heart," he said.

"Eat right, don't worry about anything, because the Bible tells us to cast our cares upon Him because He cares for us."

That's what they always reminded Ms. Martin. So she continued to do exactly what the doctor was saying and listened to her family. She was strong and healthy as a result of that.

Ms. Martin said, "Hope, you better get home, girl, and get off your feet. I know you're tired. That baby is coming real soon, so you have to get some rest, Shugga."

Hope went back home and saw cars parked all over the yard. She couldn't help but wonder, "What's happening here at this house?" She didn't quite understand what was going on, but she felt it must be something wonderful since everyone was there.

She walked in. "Surprise!" they all shouted.

Hope said, "You didn't, Mother!" She said, "Mother, that's why you weren't at church."

Her mom said, "Yay, hey, girl!"

So Hope said, "Oh, thank y'all so much. You guys are too much. Joseph, did you know anything about this?"

Joseph had this little sly grin on his face, and she said, "You knew?" He said, "Yeah."

So they began to hug and embrace one another, and Hope was so thankful and just outdone, actually. "You guys are always up to something, always doing something," she said. But she had a big support system that loved her.

Hope opened the gift, and one by one, each gift was camouflaged to prevent them from knowing the gender of the child.

After opening what Hope thought was the last gift, Ms. Lydia smiled knowingly as she and her best friend appeared carrying a large box wrapped in shiny paper. It was so big that it took both of them to bring it into the room. Everyone watched with excitement, wondering what could be inside. They brought it over to her and had Hope sit in the middle of the floor. Laughter filled the room as they gently pushed all the other gifts aside, making space for the biggest surprise of the day, the huge box that seemed almost as tall as Hope herself.

The colors were neutral; you wouldn't know if it was a boy or a girl. So she began to unwrap it. They had it wrapped really well. She had bows on top of bows. She finally got to the last bow, and then she began to take the top off.

When the top came off, a pink bunny sprang out of the box. Hope said, "Hey, wait! What's happening?"

And before she could get the pink bunny, a blue bunny jumped out of the box.

Hope said, "No! No! Not so!"

Joseph looked and said, "Yes! We are having twins!"

Hope said, "You guys have outdone yourself. Thank you. Joseph, how did you keep this secret? When I had the ultrasound, you knew all the time?"

He said, "Yes." He said, "That's why I was making sure you rested and were taking it easy."

She expressed her gratitude, saying, "Thank you. I love you all so much. Thank you so much. This truly is a blessing." Tears welled up as she reflected. "Looking back on my life, I never imagined I would reach this stage, feeling so much joy. I am grateful to God for allowing you all to share this moment with me. It's a blessing. Now, God has given me double the blessings, and I am truly thankful."

"I'm reminded of the scripture: The joy of the Lord is my strength. He's my salvation. He's my solace. He's everything I need. I thank Him for His goodness, and I thank you guys for loving me."

Hope said, "I feel like David in Psalms 27 and 13: I had fainted, unless I had believed to see the goodness of the Lord in the land of the living. Who would have thought this would be me in 2025, in this time in my life, that I have so much? I thank God for the House of Exposure that has exposed the truth in hundreds of lives. It is my sincere prayer that God will continue to bless each of you. Joseph, do you want to say anything?"

Joseph said, "Yes, but you all see the tears that flow throughout the room. All I can say is, Lord, we thank You for shining upon us. Thank You for Your grace and Your mercy, and especially for Your loving Son, who gave His life so we could be here right now. Because without that sacrifice, we couldn't have forgiven each other. We couldn't move forward without it. So we thank You, Lord, for sending Your Son, Jesus Christ, so we're able to go forth and do the things that we need to live, to love, and to make it into glory. This is truly a blessing."

He paused for a moment, looking around the room at the faces of family and friends, their eyes glistening with gratitude. "Thank you all," he continued. "Like my wife, Hope, said, we thank you from the depths of our hearts. We ask that you continue to pray for us, because we will be praying for you. And don't forget Mother Martin, she's getting better every day. Let's keep her lifted up in prayer. And again, thank you all. Be blessed, because the blessings of the Lord make us rich and add no sorrow."

And they all said, "Amen."

A month later, Hope went into labor. "Joseph, my water just broke!" she cried out.

Joseph ran into the room and said, "Let's go, let's go, let's go!"

In his excitement, he rushed out of the house, then had to come back in because he had left Hope sitting on the couch.

Hope laughed through the pain. "Joseph, slow down now. I'm the one having the baby, not you."

He smiled and said, "Okay, baby, let's go." He helped her to the car, and they headed toward the hospital.

On the way, Joseph saw something in the road, a deer that had been hit, but he whispered, "Lord, take care of that deer, because I've got to get these babies out of here."

When they arrived, Joseph ran to the emergency door shouting, "Help! My wife's in labor! She's having twins!"

EMTs hurriedly fetched a wheelchair, brought Hope inside, and nurses examined her vitals, advising her to remain calm and take deep breaths.

Hope gritted her teeth and said, "Joseph, this hurts."

He squeezed her hand and said, "Just breathe, baby. You got this." A nurse came in and said, "She's doing great! It won't be long now."

Joseph, trying to distract her from the pain, asked, "You got the names ready?"

She said, "You know I do. If it's a boy, it's going to be Joseph Lamar Wright. If it's a girl, it's going to be Grace Maureen

Wright."

He smiled. "Those are perfect. Joseph Lamar the Third. I love it."

Just as he was about to say "Third," Hope suddenly screamed loudly, filling the whole room, and in that moment, the first baby was born.

The doctor handed Joseph the scissors and said, "Dad, you want to do the honors?"

Before Joseph could finish cutting the cord, the second baby came. Baby Grace had arrived, full of life and strength.

The twins were perfect. Gracie: 6 pounds 11 ounces. Justin: 8 pounds 2 ounces. They had bright eyes, soft complexions, and the glow of pure joy.

The nurses cleaned them up and wrapped them in pink and blue blankets. Twenty minutes later, the nurse allowed the family in two at a time.

Everyone who entered the room shed tears of joy. They were beautiful, blessed, and filled with love.

The look on Joseph and Hope's faces that day was priceless as they thanked God for His blessings.

It was the summer of 2026. The twins were now six months old, bright-eyed, full of energy, and growing like weeds. They were already trying to pull up and take little steps. These twins were truly something special. They had the love of their mother and father, and the affection of everyone around them. They were precious gifts.

Hope and Joseph couldn't have been happier. Everything they had prayed for was finally coming to pass. The House of Exposure was thriving. People were being blessed, chains were being broken, forgiveness was flowing, and new mercies were created every day. It truly lived up to its name, a house where people felt free to release the burdens tugging at their hearts, to let go of bad energy, and to be renewed in spirit. It was a place to talk, to heal, and to pray.

The ministry was growing rapidly, and Hope and Joseph were even planning to open another location. Their dream was becoming reality, and the family that Hope had prayed for had become beautifully united with Joseph's family. Together, they were one big happy family.

When the twins turned one year old, sorrow entered the home. Grandma Martin passed away. The family was heartbroken, but they took comfort in knowing they had reconciled and rebuilt their bond before she left this world. Though the day was heavy with sadness, their hearts were at peace knowing they had shared love and forgiveness.

During the funeral, Joseph stood before the congregation and spoke from the depths of his heart. He shared how he had met Hope and how much he had come to love Grandma Martin, how sweet and gentle she was. "I'm so glad we all reconnected," he said. "If there's anyone here who has a problem or misunderstanding with your loved ones, please make it right. You don't know the day or the hour when either you or they may leave this world. Forgive, and you shall be forgiven. Love, and you will be loved by God."

The congregation was deeply moved. Grandma Martin's service was beautiful. When they viewed her in the casket, she looked as though she were simply asleep. A look of peace rested upon her face. She was dressed in pure white, with a lovely white hat upon her head, and her Bible gently placed between her hands.

As they began to view Grandma for the last time, Hope's mother Lydia slowly stood to her feet. Her voice trembled at first, but then grew strong and clear as she began to sing, "I shall wear a crown."

The congregation joined in softly, their voices blending in harmony. Tears filled many eyes as they sang together, hearts lifted in both sorrow and hope.

As the family walked out, united in love, holding one another close, they felt Grandma Martin's spirit surrounding them. It was as if her love lingered in the air, wrapping them in peace. She had left them a legacy of faith, forgiveness, and togetherness, a legacy they would carry forward for generations to come.

"Delight yourself in the Lord," Hope said softly, looking at her babies, "and He will give you the desires of your heart." (Psalm 37:4)

Be Blessed.

Chapter 11

The Reunion of Grace

It was the summer of 2027. The weather was perfect. It was a beautiful sunny day. Not one cloud was in the sky. Hope was sitting on her balcony, looking out, just thinking of the goodness of God.

And a thought came to her. She said, "I need to have a reunion in the House of Exposure. We have had so many good turnouts and positive feedback. We have had people to be healed, delivered, and set free. I wonder if some of those people could tell their testimonies. A testimony of grace, how the Lord has delivered them. I'm going to give this idea to Joseph so he can think about it with me. And we will pray and get this together."

Hope had a full day ahead of her. She had much work that needed to be done, so her mind was on that and many other things. However, that idea kept crossing her mind, and she couldn't let it go. It was difficult for Hope to focus that day, but she managed to get through it. Later that evening, while having dinner, she shared her idea with Joseph about what God had given her for the House of Exposure. She began to tell him what

God had spoken to her heart about, and Joseph, of course, was elated.

He was so spiritual. Joseph reminded her of a girl who went to church and turned everything into a spiritual moment. It didn't matter what it was; she found a message in it. Hope smiled because Joseph was always that way, too. He said, "That sounds like a good idea. This will help people, and we can start planning as soon as possible. We already have the contact information and everything we need. Let's make this a big and exciting day."

Hope smiled warmly and said, "Yes, Joseph. You are the best. You are so wonderful." They hugged each other happily before getting ready for dinner. Hope had prepared green beans, mashed potatoes, and meatloaf, all favorites of Joseph, although he liked almost everything! She made it with love just for him. They enjoyed a lovely evening together, and the next day, they began planning exciting new things.

Hope said, "Joseph, we need to get a planning committee for this. Let's get some of the girls who have already been established through the House of Exposure and let them help us. Of course, your mother and even your best friend, Susanna, may have ideas. Let's get a team together so we can get this taken care of. This is something I want to get done as soon as we can because I feel like it's very important and it's going to help."

A week had passed since they began planning the big event. Hope created flyers that were distributed around town and nearby areas, including on Facebook and Instagram. The message was clear: it would be an extraordinary day.

One morning, while Hope and Joseph were in the office planning for the event, a young lady came in and asked if she could see them. She had cleared it with the secretary and began to talk. She said, "I read the flyer, and I was wondering, may I be a part of your story or your testimonials? Because I can relate to this. My name is Francine, and I know what grief looks like."

Hope and Joseph said, "Yes, ma'am, thank you for coming in. It's our pleasure to have you be a part of this great celebration. May we ask a little bit about your story?" Francine began to tell them all the things she had gone through with the loss of her son. While talking, tears flowed down her face. Hope said, "Are you okay?"

Francine said, "Yes, ma'am, I'm okay. I'm in a good place right now, but it's still hard to talk about. I would love to do this if it's going to help one mother, one father, anybody who's grieving. Then it would be worth it all."

Hope said, "I understand." Joseph patted her on the back and said, "Yes, that sounds like a good idea. This is what God wants from us, to share and to help somebody else get through their pain and trouble."

The momentous occasion had finally been attained. The sun was shining brightly, the sky was clear, and a gentle breeze was flowing through the atmosphere. The House of Exposure was exquisitely adorned with subtle hues of pink, white, and gold. The tables were draped with fresh flowers, and the fragrance of elegance permeated the entire building.

Hope stood in the front of the hall, looking around with tears in her eyes. She said, "Lord, you did this. Look at what you've done." Joseph came over and put his arm around her and said, "You see? You had a vision, and you followed through. This is what obedience looks like." Hope smiled and said, "It's all God."

The people began arriving one by one. Former mentees, families, friends, pastors, and community leaders all came together to celebrate the reunion of grace. The air was filled with laughter and hugs. Everyone appeared so happy.

When it was time to start, Hope approached the microphone and welcomed everyone. She said, "Welcome, everyone. This is the day the Lord has made, and we will rejoice and be glad in it. Today, we celebrate grace, the grace that has carried us so far. You've probably heard the saying, 'If it had not been for the Lord who was on my side,' and I can truly attest to that today.

After a few songs and testimonies, Hope introduced Francine.

"Now we will hear from one of our dear sisters who has a story of grace and healing. Please help me welcome Sister Francine."

Francine walked up to the podium slowly, holding her notes, her hands trembling a little, but she smiled. She looked out across the room and said, "Good afternoon, everyone. My name is Francine, and I'm here today because of the grace of God. There was a time when I didn't think I could make it. I lost my son, my only child, and I didn't know how to live anymore. But God kept me. Through the pain, He held me together."

She paused, took a deep breath, and continued, "Coming to the House of Exposure was the turning point in my life. I met Sister Hope, and she helped me see that even in grief, there's purpose. My child's life meant something, and my story can help somebody else heal. I thank God for this house, for this ministry, and for every person in here today. Because of grace, I can smile again."

The crowd clapped; some cried, and many rose to their feet in praise. Hope wiped tears from her eyes and whispered, "Thank you, Lord, for your mercy and your grace."

After Francine finished, Lydia stood to share her testimony about mercy. A former mentee followed, offering a few words about forgiveness and the importance of keeping one's heart healthy and strong. One by one, people came forward to share how the House of Exposure had changed their lives.

Joseph stood last and stated, "This is the essence: family, faith, and forgiveness. The Scripture informs us that all matters cooperate for the benefit of those who love God. Observe this assembly. We are living evidence of that truth."

Hope smiled, took Joseph's hand, and looked around the room filled with people who had been touched by grace. She whispered, "Lord, you did it again."

After the last testimony, there was not a dry eye in the room. The people were deeply moved, their hearts overflowing with renewed hope. Everyone realized just how important and sacred the House of Exposure truly was.

Just as Joseph and Hope embraced, a man rose to his feet and said, "Excuse me."

Joseph turned toward him. "Yes, sir?"

The gentleman smiled and began to speak. "My name is Kerry Chandler. I represent Caring Americans, and we've been hearing wonderful things about this beautiful outreach. I had to come to this event in person. As the CEO of the company, I made a conscious decision to see for myself what you all are doing here. And I must say, your hard work has truly paid off. These life-changing testimonies speak volumes."

He paused, holding up an envelope. "I have a check to present in the amount of five hundred thousand dollars to aid in this endeavor. You and your team are amazing. Keep up the good work."

The crowd erupted in tears and applause. It was a moment no one in that room would ever forget.

Hope wiped her eyes, stepped forward, and took the microphone. Her voice trembled but carried warmth and strength.

"Mr. Chandler," she said softly, "from the bottom of our hearts, thank you. Your generosity means more than words can express. You've not only blessed this house, but you've also blessed every soul that will walk through its doors."

The audience stood to their feet, clapping once more as Joseph wrapped his arm around her. Together, they smiled through tears, grateful for the miracle that had just unfolded. The evening concluded with prayer, laughter, and joyful hearts. It truly felt like a reunion of grace.

May the grace of God and the sweet communion of the Holy Ghost rest, rule, and abide in us until we meet together again.

Closing Prayer

By Missionary Susie D. Liddell

May the Lord bless each person who reads or hears this book. I'm praying that God would touch you wherever you may be, whatever stage of life you are in, from childhood to adulthood. Touch, Lord. Deliver, Lord. Open the minds of Your people so they can see You and the power of Your might in the name of Jesus. Not my will, but Your will, O God.

Bless the readers, God. If they put it on Braille, bless them to feel and know that these are the words of God. Bless them, the ears that they may hear, the eyes that they may see. Let this book bless the life of a young person so they can expose anything that is happening to them in their life. Give them a safe place, God, to go in the name of Jesus.

If there is a hurting mother, Lord, touch her right where she is. A hurting father, touch him now, Father, in the name of Jesus. You are our King. You are our Lord. You are our Savior. You said that we could bring our problems to You, and You would fix them.

And God, this is the prayer that I am asking of You tonight. I believe it because Your Word says, *Ask and it shall be given; knock, and it shall be opened.* Lord, I am knocking even now. Create an atmosphere of change in the name of Jesus. Let Your Spirit abide in the name of Jesus.

This is my honest prayer, and I close it saying, *Yes, Lord.* Yes to Your will and yes to Your way. Yes, dear Father, I will obey. When I gave you a yes, I meant it from the bottom of my heart. And I say, *Yes.*

Final Reflection

May your face always show your heart. Not the thoughts of the mind, not the thoughts of people, but the thoughts that come from your heart. Because out of the heart are the issues of life.

If your heart is broken, ask God to create in you a clean heart and renew the right spirit within you, and He'll do that for you. Jesus said to forgive seventy-seven times seven per day, so that's necessary. We have to forgive and love one another.

When we forgive, we can put on the face of truth and not be a hypocrite, because God said that whether you be hot or cold, if you were lukewarm, He would spew you out. He said, "I desire truth in the inward parts," so we have to be true to ourselves and true unto God.

Until the Lord blesses me to write the next book, you be blessed, in Jesus' name.